KU-288-501

Our World

Water

Neil Morris

Chrysalis Children's Books

First published in the UK in 2002 by
Chrysalis Children's Books
An imprint of Chrysalis Books Group Plc
The Chrysalis Building, Bramley Road
London W10 6SP

Paperback edition first published in 2005

Copyright © Chrysalis Books Group Plc 2002
Text by Neil Morris

All rights reserved. No part of this book may be reproduced or utilized in any form or by any means, electronic or mechanical, including photocopying, recording or by any information storage and retrieval system, without permission in writing from the publisher, except by a reviewer who may quote brief passages in a review.

ISBN 1 84138 416 X (hb)
ISBN 1 84458 234 5 (pb)

British Library Cataloguing in Publication Data
for this book is available from the British Library.

Series editor: Jean Coppendale
Designer: Peter Clayman
Artwork: Chris Forsey
Picture researchers: Terry Forshaw, Louise Daubenay, Jenny Barlow and Ashley Brent
Consultant: Bethan Currenti

Printed in China

10 9 8 7 6 5 4 3 2 1

Picture acknowledgements:

(T) = Top, (B) = Bottom, (L) = Left, (R) = Right.

C = Corbis, CI = Chrysalis Images, CO = Collections, DV = Digital Vision, E = Ecoscene, GI = Getty Images, P = Papilio, PI = Pictor International, SPL = Science Photo Library.

Front cover (main) PI; Title Page & 18 Martin Dohrn/SPL; 4 Donald E. Carroll/GI; 5 (T) CI, (B) Ken Redding/C; 6 Bohemian Nomad Picturemakers/C; 7 (T) Ezio Geneletti/GI, (B) Rick Price/C; 8 DV; 9, front cover (inset) and 31 (L) Ben Spencer/C; 10 CI; 11 (B) Michael S. Yamashita/C; 12 & back cover (L) Richard T. Nowitz/C; 13 (T) CI, (B) Roger Wood/C; 14 (T) Janet Wishnetsky/C, (B) Paul A. Souders/C; 15 W. Cody/C; 16 Ed Kashi/C; 17 (T) Roger Wood/C, (B) & 31 (R) George Wright/CO; 19 Robert Pickett/P; 20 & back cover (R) Wiliams/E; 21 & front cover (inset) Phillip Colla/E; 22 & front cover (inset) Clive Druett/E; 23 & front cover (inset) Kevin Fleming/C; 24 W. Cody/C; 25 Larry Dale Gordon/GI; 26 James A. Sugar/C; 27 Wilkinson/E.

Contents

Water everywhere

Water is all around us. The world's oceans and seas are full of water, and they cover nearly three quarters of the Earth's surface. That is why astronauts in space see our planet as blue – it's covered in water.

Huge oceans cover the surface of our planet Earth.

Water rushes down from mountains to fill the oceans.

We need to drink lots of water to stay fit and healthy.

Water is more valuable than gold because all living things need it to stay alive. There is even water inside each of us. It makes up about two thirds of our body weight!

Liquid, solid and gas

When we talk about water, we usually mean a **liquid**. It might be running from a tap to fill a bath, or a stream flowing down a mountain, or ocean waves breaking on the shore.

Water can be great fun, which is why we learn to swim.

But the amazing thing about water is that it can change from a liquid into a **solid** or a **gas**. When it is very cold, water turns into solid ice. And when it is very hot, it changes into a gas called **water vapour**.

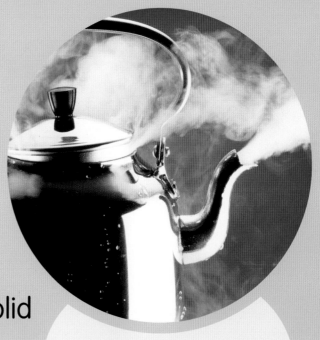

Steam from a boiling kettle is a type of water vapour.

When solid icebergs melt in warmer seas, they turn back into liquid water.

Clouds and rain

Dark, stormy clouds usually mean that rain is on its way.

Clouds are made of billions of tiny water droplets. Sometimes the water droplets in clouds join together. They become so heavy that they cannot go on floating in the sky. Then the droplets fall from the clouds to the ground.

Fluffy white clouds are blown by the wind and often move quickly across the sky.

The water droplets mainly fall as rain, which can make you very wet if you go outside without a raincoat or an umbrella. Sometimes water also falls as frozen **hail** or **snow**.

It can be fun out in the rain if you're dressed properly.

Never-ending cycle

Some of the rain that falls on high ground flows downhill in small streams. These soon join together to make rivers, which carry water to the sea.

Lakes are filled by rainwater flowing in rivers and streams.

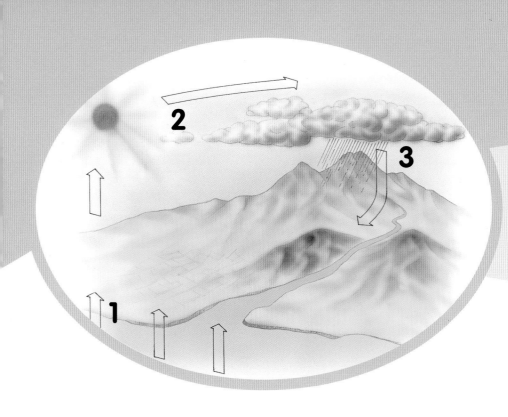

Water moves in a never-ending cycle.

1 Heat from the sun changes some of the water in the sea into water vapour. **2** This vapour rises into the air and forms clouds.

3 Then it changes back into liquid and finally falls as rain. This starts the never-ending water cycle all over again.

Rivers often twist and turn on flat land near the sea.

Salty sea

Sea water is salty, as you will know if you have ever accidentally swallowed some! But it doesn't start off that way. The rain that falls from the sky is not at all salty, so we call it fresh water.

It's easier to float on the salty sea than in the fresh water of a river or swimming pool.

As fresh water flows over land in rivers, it picks up tiny particles from rocks. These particles, called minerals, are then washed into the sea.

Rivers carry more soil, stones and mud as they get bigger and wider.

The most common mineral is the same as the salt we eat, which makes the sea taste salty.

If seawater is left in shallow **pans**, the liquid turns to vapour and leaves salt behind. This is how sea salt for cooking is made.

Using water

We use water all the time, for drinking, washing and cooking. It is also mixed with fruits and other plants, such as tea, to make drinks with different flavours. We also need water to make bread and many other foods.

Water keeps us clean and fresh.

Farmers use a lot of water to grow their crops.

These huge concrete towers are used for cooling water near a factory.

Washing machines and dishwashers use large amounts of water at home. In factories, water is often used to cool machinery, and sometimes it is turned into steam to drive machines.

safe to drink

In many places, people get their water from deep wells. Water from under ground may be pure enough to drink. In towns and cities, the water that is pumped to people's homes mainly comes from rivers and **reservoirs**.

Water is carefully tested before it is sent to our homes.

At a treatment works, water trickles down through filters to clean it.

To make it safe to drink, this water is cleaned at a **treatment works**. It passes through **filters** made of sand and **gravel**. Then chemicals are added to make sure that the water is free of harmful **bacteria**.

Treated water is pumped to our homes through large underground pipes. Sometimes these pipes burst and leak.

At the surface

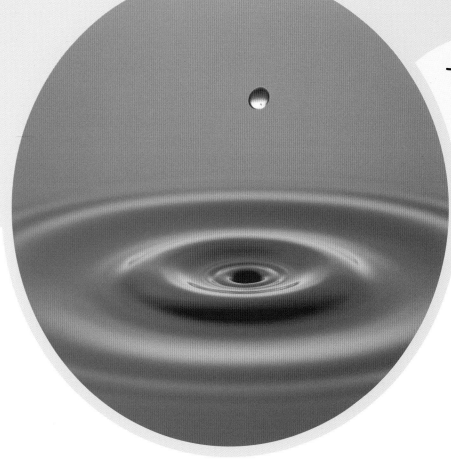

The water surface shakes and bulges when a droplet hits it.

We can't normally see it, but the surface of water is like a thin, stretchy skin. The skin is caused by surface tension, which means that the surface of the water is stretched tight.

Surface tension also causes water on a dry surface to form droplets rather than just spread out everywhere.

Some small insects are so light that they can even use surface tension to walk on water.

Living in water

Millions of different creatures live under water in oceans, lakes, rivers and ponds. Fish spend their whole lives in water. They have **streamlined** bodies, slippery **scales** and they breathe through **gills**.

Fish feed on smaller creatures that live in the water.

The blue whale is the largest creature in the world.

Other water animals, such as whales and dolphins, come to the surface regularly. They do this to breathe through their lungs. Many birds and other animals like to live close to water, where they find their food.

Keeping dry

Many materials soak up water like a sponge. If you have ever left a woolly jumper or a paper comic out in the rain, you will have seen how they become heavy with soaked-up water.

Water slips off a duck's feathers, keeping it warm and dry.

This fisherman's clothing protects him from the sea and rain.

But some materials, such as rubber and plastic, are **waterproof**. This means that they don't let water through. Outdoor clothes and umbrellas are often treated with a waxy liquid. This helps to make them waterproof.

Water power

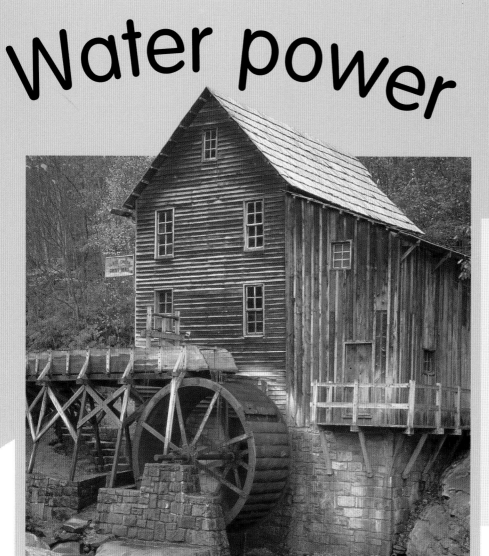

The water-wheel is joined to other wheels inside the building. These work a mill or another machine.

Throughout history people have found many ways to make water work for them. Waterwheels turn by the force of a flowing stream or river. Since ancient times, they have been used for jobs such as grinding corn.

Today, we use the power of water to make electricity by building huge **dams** across rivers. The rushing water turns the blades of a **turbine**. This drives a **generator**, which produces electricity.

Many towns and cities get their electricity from nearby river dams.

Looking after supplies

Leaks in water pipes must be mended quickly so that we don't waste water.

Water is so valuable that we must all make sure that we don't use more of it than we really need to. In some poorer parts of the world, water is already very scarce.

It is also important that the world's water is kept clean. Chemicals from factories, oil spills, sewage and our rubbish can easily **pollute** water.

We must all take great care of our rivers, lakes and other water sources and help to keep them clean.

Do it yourself

Here are some simple water experiments.

1 Put a paper clip on a small piece of kitchen paper. Then gently rest the paper and clip on water in a bowl. Soon the paper will fill up and sink, leaving the clip floating on the surface. Is it magic or surface tension?

2 Water **expands** when it freezes int ice. Fill a small bottle to the very top with water, and then cover it with foil or a milk-top. Put the bottle in a freeze and leave it until the water turns to ice The frozen, expanded ice will come out of the top and push the foil up.

3 Things float more easily in salty water. Fill a glass with water and put in a fresh egg, which will sink. Then add 3 or 4 teaspoons of salt and stir very gently. The egg will float to the surface!

Glossary

bacteria Tiny living things that can only be seen through a microscope and which can cause disease.

clouds Masses of water droplets floating in the sky.

dams Large barriers across rivers that hold back water.

expand Grow bigger and take up more space.

filters Devices that hold back dirt or unwanted material from a liquid or gas that passes through it; a sieve is a type of filter.

gas A substance, like air, that can move freely.

generator A machine that makes electricity.

gills The breathing organs of a fish, which take oxygen out of water.

gravel Lots of tiny stones.

hail Pellets of ice that fall from the sky.

liquid A substance that flows freely, like water from a tap.

minerals Solid chemical substances that occur naturally in the Earth.

pollute To damage water (or air or soil) with harmful substances.

rain Liquid drops of water that fall from the sky.

reservoirs Artificial lakes where water is stored.

snow Ice crystals that fall from the sky.

solid A substance that is hard rather than liquid and runny.

steam The gas or vapour that boiling water turns into.

streamlined Specially shaped so that water or air flows past easily.

treatment works A place where water is cleaned so that it is safe to drink.

turbine A machine with blades that are turned by moving water.

waterproof Something that keeps out water.

water vapour Water in the form of a gas that floats in the air.

index